Karin Ioannou-Naoum-Wokoun
Gerald Nestler
Martin Helmuth von Ruelling

Business Phrases for Executives
How to talk shop professionally – and succeed!

EHV

Ioannou-Naoum-Wokoun, Karin; Nestler, Gerald;
Ruelling, Martin Helmuth von

Business Phrases for Executives
How to talk shop professionally – and succeed!

ISBN: 978-3-86741-686-3
Auflage: 1
Erscheinungsjahr: 2011
Erscheinungsort: Bremen, Deutschland

© Europäischer Hochschulverlag GmbH & Co KG,
Fahrenheitstr. 1, 28359 Bremen

www.eh-verlag.de

Karin Ioannou-Naoum-Wokoun
Gerald Nestler
Martin Helmuth von Ruelling

Business Phrases for Executives
How to talk shop professionally – and succeed!

BUSINESS PHRASES FOR EXECUTIVES
from the series
Business English A – Z
is meant for those who want to:

Express themselves professionally
Interact diplomatically
Find the right wording
Sugarcoat their messages
Read between the lines

MASTER THE ART OF TALKING SHOP!

BUSINESS PHRASES

FOR

EXECUTIVES

How to talk shop professionally—

and succeed!

A collection of useful phrases by

Karin Ioannou-Naoum-Wokoun
Martin Helmuth von Ruelling
Gerald Nestler

BUSINESS ENGLISH A – Z Series

The authors would like to express their special thanks to

Sarah and Richard Graham

for their invaluable advice and assistance.

How to use this booklet:

Bold typeface in SMALL CAPS is used for example phrases:
Excuse me. Can I have a receipt, please?

Words in regular typeface are to be substituted by authentic names or situations:
My name is Martin Baron. **I run the** marketing department.

Words in italics indicate explanations:
Sorry, if you'll excuse me, I have to take this. *(Referring to an incoming call)*

Dates

3 July is pronounced **the third of July** or **July the third.**

CONTENTS

1. How to express oneself during a business trip 7

2. How to get started and socialise at a meeting 11

3. How to do small-talk 17

4. How to refer to food 19

5. How to boost your rhetorical skills 23

6. How to make arrangements 33

7. How to make telephone conversation 37

8. How to agree and disagree 47

9. How to avoid misunderstanding 53

10. How to deal with problems 57

11. How to make and deal with complaints 61

12. How to express oneself in a meeting 63

13. How to join a teleconference 77

14. How to make presentations 81

15. How to describe graphs, charts and trends 91

16. How to negotiate 95

17. How to run a formal meeting 101

HOW TO EXPRESS ONESELF DURING A BUSINESS TRIP

HOW TO WELCOME SOMEONE AT ARRIVALS

EXCUSE ME. MY NAME IS Martin Baron. YOU MUST
BE WAITING FOR ME.

EXCUSE ME. YOU MUST BE Ms Kingston.

HOW WAS YOUR flight?
DID YOU HAVE A PLEASANT journey?
WELL, I GUESS YOU MUST BE TIRED AFTER YOUR LONG flight.

HOW ARE THINGS?
HOW IS BUSINESS?

LET ME TAKE those FOR YOU.
LET ME HELP YOU WITH YOUR bags.

LET ME SEE IF I CAN GET US A TAXI.

WE'VE BOOKED YOU INTO THE Imperial IF THAT'S OK.

WE'VE BOOKED A TABLE FOR 8.30. IS THAT OK?

WE'VE BOOKED YOU ONTO A LATER return flight. IS THIS
OK FOR YOU?

How to express oneself in a taxi

OK, I'LL DROP YOU OFF AT your hotel FIRST.
SORRY, CAN YOU DROP ME OFF ON THE CORNER OF Main Street?

OK, I'LL PICK YOU UP AT eight, SHALL I?

I'LL JUST PAY THE DRIVER.
EXCUSE ME. CAN YOU CHANGE A fifty, PLEASE?

EXCUSE ME. CAN I HAVE A RECEIPT, PLEASE?

How to express oneself at the hotel check-in

I WAS WONDERING IF YOU HAD ANY ROOMS WITH A sea-view AVAILABLE?

WHAT TIME DO YOU START SERVING breakfast?
COULD I HAVE breakfast SENT UP TO MY ROOM, PLEASE?
EXCUSE ME, COULD YOU TELL ME WHAT TIME YOU STOP SERVING dinner?

EXCUSE ME. COULD I HAVE AN ALARM CALL AT half past six
TOMORROW MORNING, PLEASE?

COULD I CHANGE SOME MONEY, PLEASE?

IS THERE A bank NEAR HERE?

WHAT TIME DO I NEED TO BE OUT OF MY ROOM?

8

COULD YOU PLEASE TELL ME HOW TO GET wifi IN MY ROOM?

COULD YOU PLEASE TELL ME HOW TO GET TO the city centre ON FOOT?

COULD YOU PLEASE ORDER A taxi FOR ME?

HOW TO DEAL WITH PROBLEMS IN THE HOTEL

I'M AFRAID THE ROOM IS A BIT TOO noisy. COULD I HAVE
a more quiet ROOM, PLEASE?

I'M AFRAID THERE'S a bath-towel MISSING IN MY ROOM.
COULD YOU SEND ONE UP TO ME, PLEASE? THIS IS room 802.

COULD I HAVE an extra pillow, PLEASE? THERE SEEMS TO
BE ONE MISSING.

I'M AFRAID THERE'S NO adapter IN MY ROOM. MAY I HAVE
ONE SENT TO 108, PLEASE?

I'M AFRAID THE sewage is blocked. COULD SOMEONE
COME UP TO FIX IT ASAP, PLEASE?

I'M AFRAID THE light has gone out IN THE BATHROOM. COULD
YOU PLEASE SEND SOMEONE UP TO EXCHANGE THE light bulb?

I'M AFRAID THE TV set DOESN'T SEEM TO BE WORKING. COULD
SOMEONE COME UP AND FIX IT, PLEASE?

2

HOW TO GET STARTED AND SOCIALISE

HOW TO GREET

GOOD MORNING / AFTERNOON / EVENING.
HELLO Martin. **GOOD TO SEE YOU AGAIN.**
HI Karin. **HOW ARE YOU?**

HOW TO INTRODUCE YOURSELF

GOOD MORNING. MY NAME IS Karin Cute.
HI, I'M Sarah.

I'M FROM Hastings.

I'M WITH London Airlines.
I WORK FOR Sweet Suite Hotels.

I'M IN sales / finance / marketing.

I'M HEAD OF THE HR department.
I'M IN CHARGE OF Purchase.
I'M RESPONSIBLE FOR Sales.

I **REPORT TO** Martin.

I'**M** Gerald's **P.A.**

I've just recently started here.

HOW TO INTRODUCE A THIRD PERSON

Martin**, I'D LIKE YOU TO MEET** Karin.

Karin**, CAN / MAY I INTRODUCE YOU TO** Gerald?

Gerald**, HAVE YOU MET** Sarah **YET?**

Sarah**, DO YOU KNOW** Martin?

HOW TO TALK ABOUT YOUR COMPANY

THE COMPANY WAS STARTED IN 1968.

WE MAKE / MANUFACTURE / SELL / DISTRIBUTE chinaware.

WE HAVE FACTORIES IN Germany, the UK and China.

WE HAVE fifteen **SUBSIDIARIES / BRANCHES** worldwide.

WE HAVE A WORKFORCE OF 500.

How to refer to the weather to break the ice

A: Lovely weather, isn't it?
B: Yes, it's great / glorious, isn't it?

A: It's a bit chilly today, isn't it?
B: Yes, I guess it could be slightly warmer.

A: It's a bit cold, isn't it?
B: Yes, absolutely freezing, isn't it?

A: Isn't it a bit miserable outside?
B: Yes, you're right. I hope it's getting better soon.

A: Look at that rain! It's really coming down hard.
B: What a downpour! I hope it lets up soon.

A: It was pouring all night, but now it's just drizzling.
B: Yeah, and let's hope this is over soon, too.

A: Isn't it muggy?
B: Yes, it's very humid, isn't it?

A: The humidity is really getting to me.
B: I can imagine! It's a good thing your office is air-conditioned.

A: What oppressive weather, don't you think?
B: Yes, it's terrible. I wish a breeze would come soon.

HOW TO DESCRIBE DUTIES AND RESPONSIBILITIES

MY JOB IS TO facilitate the smooth running of events.
MY JOB INVOLVES dealing with foreign customers.
IN THIS JOB YOU HAVE to make use your soft skills.

I'M RESPONSIBLE FOR personnel matters.
I'M IN CHARGE OF the accounting department.

I RUN THE marketing department.

HOW TO RESPOND APPROPRIATELY

A: **EXCUSE ME.**
B: **YES, PLEASE? / CAN I HELP YOU?**

A: **SORRY.**
B: **SORRY.**

A: **SORRY.**
B: **NO PROBLEM / NEVER MIND / DON'T WORRY / IT'S OK.**

A: **HOW DO YOU DO.**
B: **HOW DO YOU DO.**

A: **HOW ARE YOU?**
B: **FINE, THANKS AND YOU? / NOT TOO BAD, THANKS.**

A: GOOD / PLEASED TO MEET YOU.
B: AND YOU.

A: THANK YOU.
B: YOU'RE WELCOME. / IT'S MY PLEASURE.

HOW TO TALK ABOUT COMMON INTERESTS

THAT'S INTERESTING, YOU AND Sarah SEEM TO HAVE
SOMETHING IN COMMON HERE.

I think you both really like / enjoy travelling, DON'T YOU?
OH, THAT MEANS THAT WE BOTH LIKE Indian food.

HOW TO NETWORK

WELL, CAN I GIVE YOU MY BUSINESS CARD?

ACTUALLY, I'M VERY INTERESTED IN promoting contemporary art.

WELL, ACTUALLY, I WAS WONDERING IF YOU KNOW ANYONE
WHO COULD HELP US?

WOULD YOU MIND LETTING ME HAVE THEIR CONTACT DETAILS?

DO YOU THINK I COULD CALL him AND MENTION YOUR NAME?

HOW TO INDICATE YOUR OPINIONS MORE CLEARLY

PERSONALLY / IF YOU ASK ME I THINK it's definitely
worth considering.

FRANKLY I TEND TO AGREE WITH YOU.
TO BE HONEST, I CAN'T ENTIRELY AGREE.

HOWEVER / ON THE OTHER HAND, I'm not quite sure
if it will work this way.

BY THE WAY, how is your new business partner doing?

ACTUALLY / AS A MATTER OF FACT, I'm not too convinced.

OBVIOUSLY / CLEARLY, we will have to invest some more
work into this.

FORTUNATELY / LUCKILY, there's no one else in the picture.

IN GENERAL / OVERALL, I tend to agree with your proposal.

FUNNILY ENOUGH / STRANGELY ENOUGH, there's quite a heavy
demand for this kind of product.

TO SUM UP / IN SHORT, the whole thing has proved an enormous
success.

BASICALLY / ESSENTIALLY, I'm quite surprised about the outcome.

TECHNICALLY / IN THEORY, YES, however I think we will have to
elaborate on this a bit more.

3
HOW TO DO SMALL-TALK

HOW TO START A CONVERSATION

SO, WHAT LINE OF WORK ARE YOU IN?

...AND WHERE ARE YOU BASED?

SORRY, WHO DO YOU WORK FOR?

OH, WE SEEM TO WORK IN THE SAME FIELD... MAY I GIVE
YOU MY BUSINESS CARD?

ISN'T THIS AN AMAZING PLACE?
WELL, WHAT DO YOU THINK OF THE VENUE?

ISN'T THIS WEATHER FANTASTIC / A BIT MISERABLE?

HOW TO REFER TO OTHERS

EXCUSE ME. DO YOU HAPPEN TO KNOW WHO THE GENTLEMAN
WITH the Hermès tie IS?

I THINK HE'S IN logistics.

SO, WHO DO YOU KNOW HERE?

How to refer to the conference

How are you enjoying the conference?
What do you think of the conference so far?

I think he's giving a talk on intercultural awareness.

How to refer to someone's accommodation

So...where are you staying then?
Do you know how you are getting back to your hotel yet?

How to move on or say good-bye

I'm going to get a drink from the bar. Can I get you one, too?
I'm a bit peckish. Can I also get you anything?

Sorry, if you'll excuse me a moment, I'll be right back.
Sorry, if you'll excuse me a moment, I have to make a phone call.
Sorry, if you'll excuse me, I have to take this. *(Referring to an incoming call)*

Thank you for the great talk.
It's been really nice talking to you.
So, good-bye for now. It's been a pleasure meeting you.

HOW TO REFER TO FOOD

HOW TO TALK ABOUT FOOD AT THE BUFFET

MM, THAT LOOKS NICE! WHAT IS IT?
I QUITE LIKE THE LOOK OF THIS.

HM, I WONDER WHAT'S IN IT.
DOES THIS HAVE any gelatine IN IT?

DO YOU HAVE ANYTHING vegan / vegetarian?
DO YOU HAVE ANYTHING WITHOUT meat / animal fat?

IT LOOKS LIKE SOME KIND OF dessert ONLY IT DOESN'T
seem very sweet.

I THINK I MIGHT TRY A BIT OF THAT.

HM, I DON'T FANCY IT. IT LOOKS A BIT unusual, DOESN'T IT?

A: SO, WHAT ARE YOU GOING TO HAVE?
B: I'M NOT SURE. HOW ABOUT YOU?

A: COULD YOU PASS ME ONE OF THOSE forks, PLEASE?
B: HM? OH, SURE HERE YOU ARE.

How to compliment your host

IT ALL LOOKS ABSOLUTELY DELICIOUS.

I MUST SAY, THIS RESTAURANT IS A FANTASTIC CHOICE.
HOW DID YOU DISCOVER IT?

How to describe dishes

WELL, ACTUALLY, IT'S BASICALLY a vegan soufflé.

IT COMES WITH a salad.

IT'S FULLY vegetarian.

How to recommend dishes

YOU COULD TRY THE treacle cake. IT'S THE HOUSE SPECIALITY.

IF YOU LIKE seafood, YOU'LL LOVE IT.

THE lamb's VERY GOOD HERE, IF YOU LIKE lamb.

4

HOW TO 'AVOID DISASTERS'

WELL, IS THERE ANYTHING YOU DON'T EAT?

WELL, TO BE HONEST, IT'S A BIT UNUSUAL—YOU MAY NOT LIKE IT.

WELL, IN THIS CASE WE SHOULD TRY SOMETHING ELSE MAYBE.

HOW TO BE A GOOD HOST

I'LL JUST SEE IF OUR TABLE IS READY.

SHALL WE HAVE ANOTHER drink?

IS EVERYTHING ALL RIGHT?

HOW TO ORDER THE MEAL

I'M GOING TO HAVE THE steak, PLEASE.
I'D LIKE THE vegetarian lasagne, PLEASE.
...AND ONE cauliflower cheese FOR ME, PLEASE.
YES, AND CAN I HAVE THE rhubarb crumble, PLEASE?

COULD WE HAVE A bottle of the house red, PLEASE?

HOW TO START TALKING SHOP AFTER THE MEAL

WELL, JUST A BIT MORE ABOUT this business idea of mine...

SO, GOING BACK TO WHAT WE WERE TALKING ABOUT, I think it might be a good idea to renegotiate the deal.

WELL, AS I WAS SAYING, I THINK WE SHOULD focus more on avoiding intercultural misunderstandings.

HOW TO DISCUSS PAYING THE BILL

LET ME GET THIS. MY TREAT.

THIS ONE'S ON ME. YOU PAID LAST TIME.

I INSIST...OK, LET'S SPLIT IT, THEN.

5

5

How to boost your rhetorical skills
by sugar-coating your messages

How to ask politely

Could I step in here, please?

Could you explain this in more detail, please?

Would you mind opening the window a bit?
(referring to the other person)
Would you mind me/my opening the window a bit?
(referring to oneself)

Do you think you could tell me how this idea might be implemented?

Do you mind if I get back to you a bit later?

Would you mind if I elaborated on this a bit more?

Would you mind speaking up a little, Martin?

How to request politely

If you can, could you pass this on to me, please?

If you're not too busy do you think you could take a look at it by lunchtime?

If you've got a minute could you come and see me in my office?

How to offer assistance

OK, I'll see what I can do.
OK, leave it with me.

No problem. I'll get straight on it.
OK, no problem. I'll sort something out.

How to make suggestions

We could meet up again fairly soon.
Let's meet at 10 then.

Why don't we call in another meeting?
Couldn't we postpone the meeting a bit?
I suggest we meet again next week.

I **PROPOSE THAT** we'll give it a try.
I **THINK WE SHOULD GIVE IT** a second thought.

PERHAPS / MAYBE WE COULD talk to customer service about it.

IF WE DO this **WE COULD / SHOULD** bring in a external consultant.

HAVE YOU THOUGHT ABOUT GIVING Karin **A CALL?**

HOW ABOUT CONTACTING OUR customers via direct mail?

I **RECOMMEND WE INVOLVE OUR** subsidiaries.

I **WOULD ADVISE YOU** to take another look at it.

ONE OTHER WAY OF DOING THIS WOULD BE to address the
matter more directly.

WE MAY ALSO HAVE TO RECONSIDER long delivery times.

WOULDN'T IT ALSO BE A GOOD IDEA IF we thought about alternatives?

WHAT ABOUT MEETING UP TO DISCUSS THE MATTER IN FURTHER DETAIL?

WHAT WE SHOULD ALL PROBABLY BE DOING IS setting strict deadlines.

I **ASSUME WE SHOULD** get together again **AS SOON AS POSSIBLE.**

RIGHT, BUT WHY DON'T WE call in another meeting?

I **SEE. SO THIS MEANS WE'VE GOT TO GET MORE INFORMATION THEN, RIGHT?**

I **GUESS WE NEED MORE INFORMATION ON WHERE WE'RE GOING WRONG.**

HOW TO REJECT PROPOSALS

YES, I SEE YOUR POINT AND WONDERED IF we could meet somewhere in the middle.

ONE OF THE CONSEQUENCES OF THAT MIGHT BE overtrading.

TO BE HONEST, I'M A BIT WORRIED ABOUT doing business with them again.

YES, AND... *(then simply change the subject or put forward your own view)*
THANK YOU FOR THAT. *(then move on)*

THAT IS A GREAT IDEA BUT IT REQUIRES a lot of work **AND** our time is fairly limited.

WE MAY HAVE A PROBLEM IMPLEMENTING THAT, IN THAT we are not quite familiar with the local requirements there.

SORRY, I'M NOT SURE THAT'S THE BEST IDEA. HAVE YOU THOUGHT ABOUT possible alternatives?
I'M NOT SURE I AGREE WITH YOU THERE. WHAT ABOUT giving it a second thought?

I'M AFRAID IT / THAT MAY NOT WORK. WHAT DO YOU THINK?
I'M AFRAID I'M NOT ENTIRELY SURE WHAT YOU WOULD LIKE TO ACHIEVE WITH THIS.

I CAN SEE THE POINT YOU'RE MAKING BUT HAVE YOU ALREADY CONSIDERED the latest results?
WELL, I ASSUME ANOTHER ALTERNATIVE IS TO elaborate on a plan B scenario.

How to ask for opinions

How do you feel about Martin's idea? **It's great, isn't it?**
What do you think?

What's your opinion on that?
So, what's your position on this?

Karin, **what's your view?**
Martin, **can I hear your views on** our latest advertising campaign?

How to express neutral opinions

I think you're right.
In my opinion we are doing fairly well.

Well, I'm afraid I don't really think that it would
work out that way.

To be honest, it seems to me that it's a bit too much
on the optimistic side.

Well, as I see it, we all seem to agree.
Well, as far as I'm concerned there still seems to be
more room for improvement.

**From my point of view things couldn't be any better,
could they,** Gerald?

HOW TO EXPRESS OPINIONS DIPLOMATICALLY

WELL, IT SEEMS TO ME THAT we might still have to
spend some more time on this issue.

I MEAN, I WOULD SAY THAT their performance hasn't been
too good so far, has it?

I GUESS IT WOULD BE FAIR TO STATE THAT it was a good try anyway.

TO BE HONEST, AS FAR AS I'M ABLE TO JUDGE, IT SEEMS THAT we
might find it difficult to meet the deadline.

HOW TO EXPRESS STRONG OPINIONS

WELL, AS REGARDS ME, I'M ABSOLUTELY CONVINCED THAT this
idea is going to prove a success.

I'D LIKE TO MENTION THAT IT'S MY STRONG BELIEF THAT we are
risking a bit too much here.

TO BE HONEST, THERE'S NO DOUBT IN MY MIND THAT we will
easily meet the deadlines.

WELL, I MUST SAY I FIRMLY BELIEVE THAT we are going to win this tender.

IN FACT IT'S QUITE CLEAR THAT they are more experienced
in this than we are.

HOW TO LEARN FROM PAST EXPERIENCES

PERHAPS WE CAN REVIEW PAST LEARNING POINTS ALONG THE WAY.
COULD WE REVIEW LEARNING POINTS TO DATE?

WITH HINDSIGHT, WE SHOULD HAVE / COULD HAVE thought
of this before.

I GUESS WHAT WE SHOULD HAVE / COULD HAVE DONE IS
contacting our business partners well in time.

IF WE HAD a bigger workforce, WE WOULDN'T HAVE TO
employ temps.

HOW TO INTERRUPT

SORRY TO INTERRUPT, BUT COULD I JUST SAY SOMETHING HERE?
SORRY TO INTERRUPT. CAN I JUST COME IN HERE?

EXCUSE ME, BUT CAN I JUST SAY THAT we seem to be
running out of time a bit.

EXCUSE ME, BUT WHAT I JUST QUICKLY WANTED TO SAY WAS THAT
we should move on a bit more quickly, as time rushes by.

SORRY BUT COULD I JUST FINISH WHAT I WAS SAYING?

HOW TO GET HELP FROM A COLLEAGUE

A: Martin, DO YOU THINK YOU COULD SPARE A MOMENT AND
HELP ME OUT WITH SOMETHING?
B: SURE, WHAT IS IT? / CERTAINLY, WHAT CAN I DO FOR YOU?

A: I'M CURRENTLY WORKING ON a tender for Oman.
HAVE YOU GOT ANY EXPERIENCE IN THIS?
B: YES, SOME EXPERIENCE. WHAT ARE YOU TRYING TO DO?

A: SORRY TO BOTHER YOU, BUT I'D REALLY APPRECIATE
YOUR INPUT HERE.
B: CERTAINLY, HOW CAN I HELP?

A: SORRY FOR BEING A NUISANCE, BUT I'M NOT SURE HOW / WHERE
TO START.
B: IT'S USUALLY FAIRLY STRAIGHTFORWARD, LET ME SHOW YOU.

A: I WAS WONDERING WHAT YOU THOUGHT ABOUT THIS
NEW CONCEPT.
B: I THINK IT LOOKS GOOD; IN FACT, IT COULD HELP A LOT.

A: SORRY FOR INTERRUPTING YOU BUT this computer DOESN'T
SEEM TO BE WORKING.
B: LET'S HAVE A LOOK AT IT.

5

HOW TO REQUEST INFORMATION / HELP

I WAS WONDERING WHAT YOU CAN TELL ME ABOUT
the latest board meeting.

EXCUSE ME. WHERE CAN I GET MORE INFORMATION ON
how to word this tender?

SORRY, BUT DO YOU THINK YOU COULD HELP ME WITH
this enquiry?

I WAS WONDERING IF YOU COULD HELP me drafting the
annual report?

SORRY TO BOTHER YOU, BUT WOULD YOU MIND HELPING ME WITH
the preparation of the board meeting?

CAN YOU FILL ME IN ON WHAT THEY SAID?

I SEE... AND WHAT DID she/he SAY ABOUT Sarah's idea?

OK, AND WHAT DID HE HAVE TO SAY ABOUT the performance
of the sales team?

I UNDERSTAND. COULD YOU GIVE ME AN EXAMPLE?

6

HOW TO MAKE ARRANGEMENTS

HOW TO SUGGEST TIMES AND DATES

WOULD Tuesday, 1 August **BE CONVENIENT FOR YOU?**
WOULD next Wednesday **SUIT YOU?**

COULD WE MEET ON Monday?
SHALL WE SAY NEXT weekend?

HOW ABOUT 3 July?
WHAT ABOUT 8 February?
IS 10.30 **OK?**

HOW TO ASK FOR SUGGESTIONS

WHEN WOULD SUIT YOU?

DID YOU HAVE A TIME / PLACE IN MIND?

COULD YOU LET ME KNOW BY next week **WHEN WOULD BE CONVENIENT FOR YOU?**

HOW TO SAY WE ARE UNAVAILABLE

I'M AFRAID I'M BUSY THEN.

I'M SORRY BUT I CAN'T MAKE IT THEN.

I'M AFRAID I'M TIED UP ALL next week.

I'M AFRAID I'M BACK TO BACK ON Tuesday.
IS Wednesday POSSIBLE FOR YOU?

I'M AFRAID WE'RE WORKING ON ANOTHER PROJECT UNTIL
6 December.

I'M AFRAID I'M A BIT SNOWED UNDER AT THE MOMENT.

HOW TO CHANGE ARRANGEMENTS

I'M AFRAID I CAN'T MAKE Friday. COULD WE FIX ANOTHER TIME?

WE'VE GOT AN APPOINTMENT FOR 10.30, BUT I'M AFRAID
SOMETHING'S COME UP AND I CAN NO LONGER MAKE IT, I'M SORRY.

SORRY, BUT I CAN'T POSSIBLY DO Friday, I'M AFRAID. I'M out of
the country THEN.

I'M AFRAID I CAN'T MAKE IT ON Wednesday. I'M TERRIBLY SORRY.
WHAT ABOUT Friday?

I'M AFRAID I'VE GOT TO CANCEL OUR MEETING THIS Friday. I'M SORRY.
HOW ABOUT NEXT Monday?

I'M AFRAID I WILL HAVE TO POSTPONE OUR MEETING. WHAT'S
YOUR AVAILABILITY AS OF week 21?

OR, ALTERNATIVELY, WE COULD POSTPONE IT TO Tuesday,
COULDN'T WE?

WE COULDN'T PUT THE MEETING BACK, COULD WE?

WELL, I GUESS WE COULD BRING IT FORWARD TO Monday,
COULDN'T WE?

ALL RIGHT, THEN I'LL PENCIL IN Monday. IS THAT OK?

RIGHT, SO I'LL CALL YOU BACK THIS afternoon TO CONFIRM
IF THAT'S OK?

7

HOW TO MAKE TELEPHONE CONVERSATION

HOW TO IDENTIFY YOURSELF

GOOD MORNING, Latin American Seminars Ltd.
HOW CAN I HELP YOU?

HELLO, THIS IS Karin **FROM** Business by Cultures.
I'M RINGING ON BEHALF OF Martin.

Gerald **SPEAKING.**
HELLO, Sarah **SPEAKING.**

HI Karin, **CAN YOU TALK?**
IS IT OK TO TALK?

HOW TO FIND OUT WHO THE CALLER IS

HELLO, WHO'S CALLING, PLEASE?
SORRY, MAY I HAVE YOUR NAME, PLEASE?
SORRY, COULD I TAKE YOUR NAME AGAIN?

WOULD YOU MIND SPELLING THAT FOR ME?

HELLO, IS THAT Martin?

How to state the reason for your call

Hello, this is Sarah Kingston, Head of HR at BYB. I'm calling to ask for some information, if that's possible.

Good afternoon. Karin from LAS Ltd. speaking. The reason I'm calling is your latest ad in the Guardian.

Hi, this is Martin. I'm returning your call.

I'm calling to confirm the meeting on 6 December.
I'm calling to ask if you could attend a meeting.

I'm calling about an appointment.

I'm calling to ask if you could let me have some information.

I'm calling about the advertisement for the job vacancy.

How to ask to be connected

Could I speak to Gerald Hanson, please?
I'd like to speak to Martin Baron, please.
Could you put me through to Karin Cute, please?
May I speak to Sarah, please?

Could I have the sales department, please?
May I have extension 8270, please?

How to pass the caller on to someone else

Can you hold a second? I'll just pass you on to someone who's better able to help you.

How to ask about someone else

Could you tell me when she/he'll be back, please?
Oh, I see... And when are you expecting her/him back then?

How to talk about the weather on the phone

A: So, what's the weather like where you are?
B: Lovely and warm. Let's hope it holds. What's it like at your end?

A: I heard you were having a heat wave over there.
B: Yes, and I'm so glad it's over. How about you?

A: Did you get any of those storms?
B: No, thank goodness, they passed us by.

A: What's the temperature like over there?
B: Well, it's absolutely boiling! It must be well in the 90s. *(Fahrenheit)*

HOW TO LEAVE MESSAGES

COULD I LEAVE A MESSAGE, PLEASE?
COULD YOU TAKE A MESSAGE FOR Martin, PLEASE?
COULD YOU PASS ON A MESSAGE, PLEASE?

COULD YOU ASK her/him TO CALL ME BACK, PLEASE?

COULD YOU REPEAT THAT, PLEASE?
WOULD YOU MIND READING THAT BACK TO ME, PLEASE?
COULD YOU READ THAT BACK TO ME, PLEASE?

HOW TO TAKE MESSAGES

CAN I TAKE A MESSAGE?

MAY I TAKE A MESSAGE FOR Sarah?
SHALL I TAKE A MESSAGE FOR Gerald?

WOULD YOU LIKE TO LEAVE A MESSAGE FOR Karin?

Mr. Baron HAS AN EARLY APPOINTMENT, BUT I'M AFRAID he's ONLY
EXPECTED IN AT 10.30. WOULD YOU LIKE TO LEAVE A MESSAGE FOR
him, OR SHALL I ASK him TO CALL YOU?

I'M AFRAID Ms Kingston IS IN a staff meeting UNTIL 2.30. SHALL I
ASK her TO CALL YOU this afternoon? OR CAN I HELP AT ALL?

I'M AFRAID Ms Cute IS AT lunch with a client. WE'RE EXPECTING her BACK BY two o'clock. CAN I TAKE A MESSAGE FOR her?

Mr Baron IS AT A PRESS CONFERENCE MOST OF THE morning. SHALL I ASK him TO CONTACT YOU AS SOON AS he's BACK, OR WILL YOU CALL LATER?

HOW TO ASK FOR INFORMATION

COULD I ASK WHO'S CALLING, PLEASE?

MAY I HAVE YOUR EMAIL-ADDRESS, PLEASE?

HOW TO CHECK INFORMATION

I'M AFRAID I COULDN'T QUITE CATCH THAT. COULD YOU SPELL THAT FOR ME, PLEASE?

SO, THAT'S 1 August IF I UNDERSTOOD YOU CORRECTLY.

MAY I READ THAT BACK TO YOU?

How to offer help

I'M AFRAID she's NOT AVAILABLE TODAY. CAN I HELP YOU?

I'M AFRAID he's VISITING a client AT THE MOMENT.
CAN I TAKE A MESSAGE?

How to promise action

I'LL PASS THE MESSAGE ON TO her AS SOON AS she's BACK.

I'LL ASK her TO CALL YOU AS SOON AS POSSIBLE.
YES, I'LL ASK her TO GET BACK TO YOU AS SOON AS SHE CAN.

OK, I'LL LET her KNOW THAT YOU RANG.

OK, I'LL SEE IF I CAN REACH her/him ON her/his MOBILE.

OK, I'LL DO THAT RIGHT AWAY.

OK, I'LL SEE WHAT I CAN DO.
OK, I'LL SORT SOMETHING OUT STRAIGHT AWAY. SORRY FOR
THE INCONVENIENCE.

SORRY, CAN I GET BACK TO YOU ON THAT, PLEASE? I'LL NEED TO
GET SOME FURTHER INFORMATION.

OK, I'LL GET BACK TO YOU FIRST THING IN THE MORNING.

OK, I'LL CALL BACK LATER.
OK, I'LL SPEAK TO YOU LATER THEN.

OK, I'LL WAIT TO HEAR FROM YOU THEN.

How to avoid misunderstandings

SORRY, COULD YOU SPEAK UP A LITTLE, PLEASE?

SORRY, COULD YOU SPELL THAT FOR ME, PLEASE?

SORRY, COULD YOU SAY THAT AGAIN, PLEASE?

SORRY, COULD YOU HOLD ON A MOMENT, PLEASE?

JUST TO BE ON THE SAFE SIDE: CAN I JUST CHECK THAT
WITH YOU, PLEASE?

I MAY NOT HAVE BEEN VERY CLEAR. WERE YOU ABLE TO GET ALL OF THAT?

How to respond

THAT'S FINE / OK FOR ME.

NO PROBLEM.

How to show interest

Really?

I see.
Right.

Uhuh.

Good.
Great.

That's interesting.

How to indicate interruptions

Would you mind holding for a moment?

I'm sorry, I've got someone on the other line. Can I call you back, please?

Sorry about that. Where were we?

HOW TO INDICATE THE END OF A CALL

CAN I CALL YOU BACK in a few minutes, PLEASE?

I'M AFRAID I HAVE TO GO NOW, SOMETHING'S COME UP. I'M SORRY.

I'LL HAVE TO GO, I'M AFRAID.

I'VE GOT TO RUN BUT I'M LOOKING FORWARD TO SEEING YOU
ON 8 February.

ANYWAY, I WON'T KEEP YOU ANY LONGER. SPEAK TO YOU SOON.

WELL, I WON'T KEEP YOU ANY LONGER. I'M SURE YOU'RE VERY BUSY.

WELL, I'LL LET YOU GET ON. SPEAK TO YOU LATER.

ANYWAY, LOOK, I MUST LET YOU GO NOW.

GOOD. SO, I'LL SEE YOU ON THE 8th THEN.

RIGHT / OK THEN.

THAT'S GREAT. I'LL SEE YOU SOON THEN.

THANKS A LOT FOR YOUR HELP.

SPEAK TO YOU SOON.

THANK YOU. GOODBYE.

BYE NOW.

How to prepare the listener for a message on the voicemail

This is Martin Baron **from** Latin American Seminars.
It's 9.30 **on** Wednesday morning.
I'm ringing about the sales report.

How to leave clear contact information on the voicemail

I'm in London **until** Friday.
My telephone number is 346 766.

HOW TO AGREE AND DISAGREE

HOW TO AGREE STRONGLY

YES, I ENTIRELY / TOTALLY AGREE (WITH YOU).
THAT'S EXACTLY MY POINT.
IN MY VIEW, THAT'S PRECISELY THE ISSUE.

I DEFINITELY AGREE WITH WHAT she/he SAID ABOUT the
London subsidiary.

YES, EXACTLY! I GUESS THERE'S NO QUESTION THAT they are
doing a great job.

I'M EXACTLY OF THE SAME OPINION!
I COULDN'T AGREE MORE!

YES, THAT'S TRUE.
THAT'S COMPLETELY / ABSOLUTELY RIGHT.

PRECISELY / ABSOLUTELY / EXACTLY!

THAT'S A GOOD IDEA.
THAT'S NOT A BAD IDEA!

I MUST SAY I THINK THAT'S THE BEST WAY OF DOING IT.

YOU'RE RIGHT – WE NEED TO ACT ON THIS NOW!

How to agree neutrally

Well, I think so, too.

I would support that.

Actually, I agree with the point about investing more time in language training.

Well, I must say I tend to agree with you there.

Well I have some reservations about this approach, but I think I can go along with it.

Actually, I'm not entirely convinced, but I'll go along with the decision.

How to agree partially

Well, I would tend to agree with you on that issue provided that we can stick to our budget.

Well, I guess by and large I would accept your views if we didn't have to set up new guidelines.

Well, although I do agree with quite a number of points you raised, I must say I do find it difficult to agree with you on the issue of job-sharing.

HOW TO SUGARCOAT DISAGREEMENT

I TAKE YOUR POINT, BUT have you considered intensified language coaching?

THAT MAY BE TRUE, BUT DON'T YOU THINK having more telcos might be quite helpful?

I SUPPOSE THAT COULD BE TRUE. HOWEVER, I THINK it will still need some time till we get there.

THAT'S TRUE, BUT HAVE YOU THOUGHT ABOUT taking on external consultants?

IN PRINCIPLE I AGREE WITH YOU, BUT I'm not entirely sure that this is the only solution.

I ACCEPT THAT, BUT I am not entirely sure about the outcome.

WELL, FRANKLY SPEAKING, I BELIEVE THAT we should give this idea a second thought.

WELL, WITH RESPECT, I'm not entirely convinced.

I AGREE WITH YOU TO A CERTAIN DEGREE BUT I think we should also consider alternatives.

I SEE / KNOW WHAT YOU MEAN, BUT don't you think we had better give it a try nevertheless, Martin?

I DON'T QUITE GET YOUR POINT HERE.

YOU HAVE A POINT THERE BUT I'm afraid I can't still really see any profit in it.

WELL, I AGREE WITH YOU UP TO A POINT. HOWEVER, I'm not entirely in favour of this idea.

I CAN SEE YOUR POINT OF VIEW, BUT I'm not yet convinced it's the best solution for us.

I'M NOT SURE I ENTIRELY AGREE WITH YOU ON THAT.

I'M AFRAID I DON'T COMPLETELY AGREE WITH YOU ON THAT ISSUE, BECAUSE I believe we still might have too little experience in this field.

How to disagree directly

I think that's beside the point, really.
It seems to me you're missing the point a bit here.

That's not really the point I'm afraid.
That's really not the point at all I'm afraid.

I'm afraid I seriously question the point about downsizing the workforce to such an extent.

I'm afraid I don't see it that way.
I'm afraid I don't really share your view on this.
I'm afraid I can't entirely share your point of view on this issue.

No, I don't really think so. Actually I'm sure it won't prove a success in the end.

I'm afraid I can't really agree with that at all.
I'm afraid I can't help feeling that we will have to disagree here.

Yes, but on the other hand I can already see a few problems related to this change.

Look, I share your concerns, but that's the position I'm afraid.

Maybe, but I think it's still too early to say.

I'm afraid I will have to disagree with the point about changing our advertising line.

I'm afraid we seem to disagree here.

I'M AFRAID I CAN'T AGREE AS TO MY UNDERSTANDING, WHAT YOU FAIL TO TAKE ACCOUNT OF IS the entirely different culture we are going to deal with.

I'M AFRAID I TOTALLY DISAGREE WITH THE POINT ABOUT reducing the number of staff.

I'M AFRAID I TOTALLY DISAGREE ON THAT POINT.

I'M AFRAID WE WILL HAVE TO AGREE THAT WE DISAGREE.

How to avoid misunderstanding

How to ask for clarification

What exactly are you saying?

Are you saying that the situation has changed that much?

Are you saying we need to relocate fairly soon?

What did you have in mind when you said we need to change our approach?

Do you mean that their performance was fairly poor?

Which means that we should stop expanding, right?

How do you mean?

Sorry, in what way do you mean that the results were a bit disappointing?

When you say you want to relocate **do you think that** our premises aren't big enough anymore?

I'm not quite sure what you mean by that.

You don't think that we should stop this project, do you?

WHAT CAN WE DO?

HOW ABOUT calling it a day?

WHAT ARE WE GOING TO DO THEN?

CAN YOU EXPLAIN IN MORE DETAIL, PLEASE?

SORRY, I DON'T QUITE FOLLOW.

SORRY, I'M NOT SURE I UNDERSTAND. WOULD YOU MIND REPEATING THAT?

I'M AFRAID I DIDN'T QUITE GET THAT. COULD YOU JUST SAY THAT AGAIN?

HOW TO CLARIFY

IN FACT, WHAT I MEAN IS that this would cause considerable delays.

I SUPPOSE WHAT THIS MEANS IS that we will have to find a new supplier.

IN OTHER WORDS WHAT I'M SAYING IS that this was not really what I had expected.

TO BE HONEST, WHAT I WAS THINKING WAS to verify all conditions in detail.

TO BE MORE SPECIFIC I WOULD SAY we should not waste too much time on this.

THE POINT I'M TRYING TO MAKE IS that there are always alternatives.

SO, IN OTHER WORDS, WE have not decided that yet.
WELL, TO PUT IT ANOTHER WAY we had better move on fast.

SORRY, I'M PROBABLY NOT MAKING MYSELF CLEAR. BASICALLY, WHAT I'M TRYING TO SAY IS that we should not focus on this issue too long.
SORRY. ALLOW ME TO REPHRASE THAT.

JUST TO CLARIFY: I do believe we are doing fairly well here.
SORRY, PERHAPS I DIDN'T MAKE MYSELF CLEAR. WHAT I MEANT TO SAY was that there's still some room for improvement in this field.

WITH RESPECT, YOU DON'T QUITE SEEM TO UNDERSTAND WHAT I WAS TRYING TO SAY. I SAID THAT this needs a bit more time.

HOW TO ASK FOR CONFIRMATION

SORRY, BUT WOULD I BE CORRECT IN SAYING THAT you are not too sure about the results yet?

JUST TO BE ON THE SAFE SIDE: WERE YOU SAYING THAT you'd miss the deadline by 2 weeks?

SO, BASICALLY, WHAT YOU ARE SAYING IS that there is still considerable work involved.

I'M NOT SURE I FOLLOW. DID YOU SAY THAT you had forgotten about the tender?

How to ask what someone has just said

Sorry, I missed that. Could you say that again, please?
Sorry, I didn't quite catch that. Could you repeat it more slowly, please?

Sorry, I didn't quite understand your point. Could you explain in a little more detail what you mean?

Sorry, I'm not entirely with you. Could you go over that again, please?

Sorry, I can't quite follow you. Could you run through that again, please?

Sorry, I don't quite see what you mean. Could you be a bit more specific, please?

How to query information you are not so sure about

Ok, let me get this right. Are you saying that your taxi got stuck in the traffic and you therefore missed the flight?

My concern about that is that we might not make it in time.

If I understand what you were saying, are you sure that this advertising campaign is in line with all the rest?

Are others in agreement with this?

How to deal with problems

How to define the problem

OK, the way I see it the problem basically is that the implementation of your suggestion would take rather long.

Well, I think there are three main aspects **to the problem.**

How to brainstorm ideas

Shall we brainstorm possible solutions to this issue? Right, let's keep the ideas coming.

OK, may I ask you what you all have to say.

Well, what if we changed our approach a bit?

Another option would be to outsource this service.

Supposing we were prepared to do so, would we profit from it accordingly?

I guess alternatively, we could have the next seminar at your headquarters.

How about changing our approach altogether?

The answer could be to increase the number of sales staff.
Why don't we take on another P.A.?

Couldn't we just launch a new product?

Well, what about being more assertive?

OK, maybe it's time to think of alternatives.

How to review ideas

OK, let's see what we've got so far.

**Well, the way I see it there are several ways we
could deal with this.**
I assume we have a number of options here / now.

I'm afraid we won't be using this idea just now.

How to select the solution

I assume on balance we should go with Martin's proposal.

OK, so how do we implement this?

HOW TO BALANCE ARGUMENTS

RIGHT, SO LET'S LOOK AT THE PROS AND CONS.

ON THE ONE HAND we need to invest some more time.
ON THE OTHER HAND we need to stick to the deadlines.

OK. LET'S DISCUSS THE ADVANTAGES AND DISADVANTAGES FIRST.

HOW TO CHANGE YOUR APPROACH

I SEE, BUT LET'S BRIEFLY LOOK AT THIS FROM ANOTHER ANGLE.

RIGHT, BUT LET'S LOOK AT THIS IN A DIFFERENT WAY.

HOW TO CONSIDER LESS OBVIOUS OPTIONS

OK, BUT DON'T YOU THINK IT MIGHT BE WORTH CONSIDERING
new alternatives?

WELL, I ASSUME WE COULD ALSO TRY it the other way round.

How to discuss possible effects

WELL, TO BE HONEST, IF WE DO THIS, we will definitely encounter new challenges.

I SEE, BUT LET'S THINK ABOUT THE CONSEQUENCES OF setting up another branch.

How to make a decision

IN MY VIEW, THE BEST WAY FORWARD IS to stick to the guidelines.
WELL, MY SOLUTION WOULD BE TO implement our ideas asap.

How to state future action

THE WAY I SEE IT THE NEXT THING TO DO IS to call in another meeting.

I ASSUME WHAT WE'VE GOT TO DO NOW IS inform our colleagues about this.

11

How to make and deal with complaints

How to make a complaint

I'm ringing to complain about the noise in the room next door.

I'm sorry, but I'm afraid I'm not satisfied with the quality of food you are serving here.

I'm afraid it really isn't good **enough.**

Unfortunately, there seems to be a problem with internal communication channels.

I'm afraid the minibar **doesn't work.**

I'm afraid we haven't received the shipment **yet.**

Sorry, but I'd really like to know why there has been such a delay.

I'm afraid if you don't replace the product immediately, **I'll** complain to the manager.

I'm afraid if you can't deliver **on time, we'll have to contact other** suppliers.

HOW TO SHOW UNDERSTANDING

OH DEAR! I'M TERRIBLY SORRY TO HEAR THAT.
I'M VERY SORRY ABOUT THE PROBLEM / DELAY.
MMM, I SEE WHAT YOU MEAN.

HOW TO GET THE FACTS

I'M TERRIBLY SORRY TO HEAR THAT. COULD YOU GIVE ME SOME
DETAILS, PLEASE?
I'M TERRIBLY SORRY TO HEAR THAT. WHAT HAPPENED EXACTLY?
I'M TERRIBLY SORRY TO HEAR THAT. WHAT'S THE PROBLEM EXACTLY?

HOW TO MAKE EXCUSES / DENY RESPONSIBILITY

I'M AFRAID THAT'S NOT QUITE RIGHT.
I'M AFRAID IT'S NOT OUR POLICY TO replace items.
I'M AFRAID IT'S NOT OUR FAULT THAT it hasn't arrived. I AM SORRY.

HOW TO PROMISE ACTION

OK, I'LL LOOK INTO IT RIGHT AWAY.
RIGHT. I'LL CHECK THE DETAILS AND GET BACK TO YOU.

How to express oneself in a meeting

How to start a meeting

Did you have a nice journey?
Was it easy to find?

OK, so let's get down to business then.
Right, can we get started, please?
Right, I think we should make a start.

Welcome to the meeting, everyone.

How to set objectives

The purpose of this meeting is to discuss last year's performance.
The aim of this meeting is to clarify possible misunderstandings.
Well, our aim is to allocate the tasks more precisely.
Do we all agree that the key issue of today's meeting is
the drafting of our new guidelines.

So today we're here to decide whether we are proceeding the
way we have done so far **or not.**

I think we should clarify our objective **today.**

HOW TO ASK FOR REACTIONS

So, Karin, WHAT ABOUT YOU?
So, Martin, WHAT ARE YOUR VIEWS?
Sarah, HOW DO YOU FEEL ABOUT THAT?
Karin, WOULD YOU LIKE TO COMMENT ON THAT?
WELL, (SO) WHAT DO YOU THINK, Gerald?

I SEE, BUT WHAT DO YOU THINK ABOUT THE IDEA OF involving
our French partners?

Martin, PLEASE FEEL FREE TO EXPRESS YOUR thoughts ON...
Karin, WHAT DO YOU THINK ABOUT Gerald's IDEA?
OK, Sarah, SO WHERE EXACTLY DO YOU STAND ON THIS ISSUE?
Martin, I WAS WONDERING WHERE YOU STOOD ON THIS QUESTION.

RIGHT. DOES ANYONE HAVE ANY SUGGESTIONS?

SORRY, I DON'T QUITE SEE WHAT YOU MEAN. WOULD YOU MIND
SAYING THAT AGAIN?

RIGHT, SO CAN YOU BRING US UP TO DATE?
COULD YOU GIVE US THE BACKGROUND, PLEASE?

I SEE, SO WHERE DO WE STAND?

I GUESS ONE OPTION WOULD BE voting on this issue, WOULDN'T IT?

WHAT IS THE BEST WAY TO PROCEED? SHOULD WE summarize
what has happened so far?

COULD YOU REPORT BACK TO ME ON THAT AS SOON AS POSSIBLE?

HOW TO RUN A MEETING

WELL, I WAS WONDERING… CAN EVERYONE KEEP THINGS SHORT AND SIMPLE?

OK, LET'S TRY TO KEEP THINGS CONSTRUCTIVE THEN, SHALL WE?

SO WHAT DO YOU THINK, Karin?

THAT'S AN EXCELLENT POINT, Martin.

BY THE WAY, I WANTED TO TALK TO YOU ABOUT our last board meeting. INCIDENTALLY, I WANTED TO HAVE A WORD WITH YOU ABOUT our sales strategy.

RIGHT. PERHAPS WE CAN COME BACK TO THIS LATER. OK, SO LET'S MOVE ON.

RIGHT, I SUGGEST WE work in small groups.

WELL, MAYBE WE SHOULD TAKE a short break and carry on afterwards.

Sarah, I'M COUNTING ON your getting us the contract, OK?

BUT Martin, I'M AFRAID THIS IS NOT THE TIME TO take on more work.

RIGHT. HAVE YOU MANAGED TO SORT OUT THE PROBLEMS WITH the purchasing department YET?

I'M AFRAID THAT'S A DECISION WE CAN'T PUT OFF ANY LONGER. I'M AFRAID I DON'T THINK IT'S HELPFUL TO MAKE THIS PERSONAL. WHY DON'T WE TAKE A TIME OUT?

SORRY BUT I THINK WE HAD BETTER TAKE A TIME OUT. I'M AFRAID
WE'RE ALL GETTING A BIT TOO EMOTIONAL HERE.

SO, I GUESS THAT'S IT AND WE'RE GOING AHEAD WITH the next
point on our agenda.

HOW TO SET PRIORITIES

AS FAR AS I'M CONCERNED IT IS IMPERATIVE THAT we launch
our campaign asap.

TO OUR UNDERSTANDING THE MOST IMPORTANT THING IS:
KISS—Keep It Short and Simple.

ABOVE ALL, I THINK WE MUST keep our core customers in mind.
TO MY UNDERSTANDING IT IS PARTICULARLY IMPORTANT TO meet
all respective targets.

I ASSUME IT IS ESPECIALLY IMPORTANT TO EXPRESS our priorities
clearly and well in time.
WELL, I GUESS IT IS IMPORTANT TO REALISE THAT we need to take
the relevant steps now.
TO BE HONEST I THINK IT IS NECESSARY TO review our marketing
strategies.

I BELIEVE IT IS CRUCIAL THAT we all entirely agree on that before
moving on.
WELL, THE MOST IMPORTANT POINT SEEMS TO ME THAT we are
all in line.

How to present one's opinion

To my understanding it's essential to realise that we need to work on our profile even more carefully.

I must say I think that this is a major issue.

I believe this point to be of the utmost importance if it comes to eventually taking on new staff.

I strongly believe we must not underestimate the impact of the current economical situation.

Let me say that I guess it's worth noting that the exchange rates are rather volatile at the moment.
At this point I would like to highlight the fact that we have been quite successful so far.

I'm afraid we cannot overlook the fact that there are quite a few foreign competitors, too.
May I just briefly draw your attention to the fact that our turnover has slightly increased recently.

Well, at this point I would like to remind you that we must closely stick to our agenda.

I'm afraid I'm not totally convinced that your suggestion is worth implementing.

Sorry to say, but to my understanding this point is, after all, only of secondary importance.

How to speed up

Sorry but I think we should move on a bit now.
OK, that was item one. Now let's move on to item two.
I think we've covered this issue thoroughly. Let's move on now.

So, what's the best way to progress this discussion?

I'm afraid I think we need to come to a decision now.

How to slow down

Let's look at this in more detail, shall we?
Well, I think we should discuss this a bit more, don't you think?

How to interrupt

Sorry, just a moment. Did you say we are no longer
the number 1 in this field?

Sorry but can I just stop you there for a moment?
Can I just come in here?
Sorry, can I just say something?

Sorry to interrupt again but I'm afraid I missed your point there.
Sorry, I don't want to interrupt but I'm afraid I couldn't quite catch that.

HOW TO TAKE THE FLOOR

IF I COULD JUST COME IN HERE.
I'D JUST LIKE TO MAKE A FEW COMMENTS ON Sarah's suggestions
IF NOBODY OBJECTS.
SORRY, BUT I HAVE A POINT TO MAKE HERE.

HOW TO COMMENT

SORRY, BUT I MAY BRIEFLY COMMENT ON THE LAST POINT THAT
HAS BEEN MADE?

EXCUSE ME, BUT I THINK IT MIGHT BE RELEVANT TO KNOW THAT
the situation is yet unchanged.
EXCUSE ME, BUT MAY I JUST DRAW YOUR ATTENTION TO THE FACT
THAT we are still the market leaders in this field.
SORRY, CAN I JUST POINT OUT THAT we seem to be running behind
schedule a bit.
SORRY, BUT I THINK IT'S WORTH ADDING THAT we are still
expanding nevertheless.

HOW TO DEAL WITH INTERRUPTIONS

SORRY, BUT COULD YOU LET her/him FINISH, PLEASE?
SORRY BUT COULD YOU JUST HANG ON A MOMENT, PLEASE

SORRY, COULD I JUST FINISH WHAT I WAS SAYING?
NOW, JUST HOLD ON A MINUTE, Karin. WHAT I WAS SAYING WAS
THAT WE would need a bit more time to implement this.

WITH RESPECT, IF YOU WOULD ALLOW ME TO CONTINUE
what I was just saying.

HOW TO KEEP TO THE POINT

WELL, HONESTLY, I'M NOT QUITE SURE THAT'S RELEVANT.

SORRY BUT COULD WE POSSIBLY GET BACK TO THE POINT LATER?
I THINK WE'RE DIGRESSING A LITTLE HERE. I'M AFRAID WE SHOULD
REALLY MOVE ON.

I'M AFRAID THAT'S COMPLETELY OUT OF THE QUESTION AT THE MOMENT.

SHALL WE get back to this point later?

HOW TO GET BACK TO THE SUBJECT

WELL, AS I WAS SAYING there's still some room for improvement.

OK, COMING BACK TO WHAT I WAS SAYING I think we are on the
right way.

ANYWAY, GETTING BACK TO THIS SUGGESTION OF MINE, WHAT I WAS
THINKING WAS THAT we should bring in some external consultants.

WE WERE ORIGINALLY TALKING ABOUT last year's turnover.
CAN WE GET BACK TO THAT?

SORRY BUT DO YOU THINK WE CAN COME BACK TO THAT?

TO BE HONEST, WE HAVEN'T REALLY FOUND OUT EXACTLY WHAT
THE problem IS YET. WOULD YOU MIND TELLING US AGAIN?

HOW TO BRING IN A SECOND PERSON

MAY I BRING IN Mr Baron WHO IS FAMILIAR WITH THIS ANALYSIS
IN MORE DETAIL THAN I AM.

I'D LIKE TO ASK MY COLLEAGUE Sarah WHO IS THE LADY IN CHARGE
OF THIS ISSUE TO DEAL WITH THIS MATTER.

Karin, SINCE YOU ARE THE EXPERT IN THIS FIELD, MAY I ASK
YOU TO KINDLY GIVE ME YOUR VIEWS ON THAT?

AT THIS POINT I WOULD LIKE TO INVITE Gerald TO PRESENT US
WITH HIS VIEWS.

WELL, AS REGARDS THIS, ALLOW ME TO GIVE THE FLOOR
TO Ms Cute.

How to make proposals

Right, so I'd propose that we take a short break.

Sorry, but I'd like to put forward the proposal that we all decide on our priorities.

In fact my proposal is that everyone voices her/his concerns.

How to make recommendations

Well, actually, we strongly recommend you to stick to the guidelines.

Actually, in our opinion it is high time that we define the right procedure.

We would actually thoroughly recommend you to take a close look at our priorities.

How to express support

Well, to be honest, I would give my full backing to Martin's suggestion.

Actually, I wouldn't be opposed to that.

I MUST SAY I'M IN FAVOUR OF Gerald's idea.
IF YOU ASK ME, I'M FULLY IN FAVOUR OF Karin's contribution.
WELL, I WOULD SUPPORT Sarah **PROVIDED THAT** you think
it's really manageable.

MY FIRST REACTION IS FAVOURABLE, BUT HAVE YOU CONSIDERED
the very last point?

HOW TO EXPRESS RESERVATIONS

WELL, I THINK WE SHOULD GRANT OURSELVES A BIT MORE TIME
BEFORE MAKING A FINAL DECISION.

SORRY, BUT I REALLY CAN'T HELP FEELING THAT it won't work out.

SORRY, BUT I MUST SAY I HAVE CERTAIN RESERVATIONS ABOUT
the very last point.

TO BE HONEST, I'M A BIT WORRIED ABOUT missing the deadlines.

HOW TO EXPRESS OPPOSITION

I'M AFRAID I CAN'T SUPPORT this proposal.

I'M AFRAID I CAN'T GIVE your suggestion **MY ENTIRE SUPPORT**
unless we slightly amend it.

To be honest, I'm not quite sure if this proposal is feasible.
I'm afraid I'm totally opposed to that idea.
To be honest, this seems out of the question to me.

I must say I'm afraid this leaves a great deal to be desired.
I'm really sorry.

How to put issues to a vote

Good, let's put that to a vote.
Who is in favour of item number 1?
Can we have a show of hands?

Thank you. Ok, that's everyone. That's agreed then.

How to summarise

OK, let's go over what we've agreed, shall we?

Let's just revise: Do we agree that the key issue is to focus on the Chinese market?

May I just go over the major points that have been expressed so far?

May I briefly summarize the issues that have been made so far?

Right, to sum up then, I would say that this has been a highly productive meeting.

So, am I right to assume that the solution is then to diversify.

OK, at this point I would like to sum up our discussion.

In short: This has been a very fruitful discussion.

Let me just briefly remind you that the points that have been made are to be implemented asap.

Well, it seems that on balance we feel we should focus on domestic suppliers.

So, what we've agreed, then, is to proceed as usual.

How to end a meeting

I think that's as far as we can go today. Thank you for a very productive meeting.

Ok. It's nearly four o'clock, I'm afraid we're running a bit short of time.

I'm afraid we'll have to break off here.

Well, as things stand now, I'm afraid we shall have to break off these negotiations. I'm sorry.

WOULD ANYBODY LIKE TO RAISE A POINT THAT WE HAVEN'T HAD
TIME TO DISCUSS?

WE REALLY MUST FIX UP ANOTHER MEETING TO DISCUSS
the open points.

HOW TO PLAN THE NEXT MEETING

OK, SO THE NEXT THING TO DO IS find a date that suits everyone.

RIGHT, SO WHAT WE'VE GOT TO DO NOW IS fix an appropriate venue.

OK, LET'S ALLOCATE RESPONSIBILITIES NOW.

Gerald, WOULD YOU LIKE TO DEAL WITH the booking of the venue?

THEN we need to send out invitations. Martin,
CAN WE LEAVE THAT TO YOU?

AND I'LL SORT OUT THE guest speakers THEN.

SO CAN WE SCHEDULE THE NEXT MEETING FOR 8 February?

How to join a teleconference

How to open a teleconference

OK, let's get started.

Hi everybody. How are you?

Hi, can I ask who's in the conference?

Hello everyone, thanks for calling in today.

Did you all get a copy of the agenda?

How to manage the agenda

As you can see, we have quite a bit to get through today.

I suggest we leave item one on our agenda until
the next session.

Let's move straight on to item two.

How to interrupt

Sorry to interrupt, but I think **we are** slightly diverting from the topic now.

Could I just come in here?
Sorry, but I'd just like to say something here.

I'm afraid I didn't quite catch that.

How to handle the procedure

As we only have little **time today, could we keep our comments brief?**

Is everyone OK with keeping our comments brief?

Some of us need to finish soon, so shall we have a focused meeting?

Sorry, could you speak one at a time?

HOW TO SHOW INTEREST / SURPRISE

REALLY?
I'M SURPRISED TO HEAR THAT.

DO YOU? / DID YOU? / DIDN'T I? / ARE YOU? / HAVE YOU? / HAVEN'T WE?

HOW TO ASK FOLLOW-UP QUESTIONS

So, Martin, WHAT DID YOU THINK OF Gerald's suggestion?

WHAT ABOUT YOU, Karin? WHEN ARE YOU GOING TO step in?

Mr Baron, HOW DO YOU FEEL ABOUT that?

HOW TO MANAGE THE DISCUSSION

So, JUST TO RECAP ON WHAT WE'VE SAID...

So, CAN WE ALL AGREE ON THAT?

ARE THERE ANY COMMENTS ON THAT?

WOULD ANYONE WISH TO COMMENT ON THAT?

How to stick to the time limit

I'd like to be finished by 10.30, if that's OK.

I'm afraid we're running short of time. What do we really need to deal with today?

Sarah, Gerald, can I leave that with you?

How to close

I think we've covered everything for now.

I'm afraid we'll have to finish here / there.
We'll have to stop here / there. Thanks everybody.

Thank you very much for your valuable input / contributions.

How to use the speaker's words in a follow-up question

A: So the meeting has been postponed until next March.
B: Next March?

How to make presentations

How to get started

.

Right... Can everybody hear me OK?
So, can everybody hear me?

Right, let's get started.

How to introduce yourself

Hello everyone, welcome to our AGM. *(annual general meeting)*

Good morning, everyone. It's good to see that so many of you were able to attend my presentation this morning. Some of you may know me already, but allow me to introduce myself.

On behalf of myself and Business by Cultures Ltd., I'd like to welcome you. My name is Martin Baron.

So, let me start by introducing myself.

Hi everyone, I'm Sarah Kingston. Good to see you all.
Hi, for those of you who don't know me yet, my name is Gerald Hanson.

GOOD MORNING. I'M VERY HAPPY TO HAVE BEEN INVITED TO TALK
TO YOU ABOUT intercultural misunderstandings. MY NAME IS
Martin Baron AND I RUN Business by Cultures IN COOPERATION
WITH Karin Cute.

HOW TO INTRODUCE THE TOPIC

AS YOU KNOW, I'M HERE TO introduce you to the topic of
intercultural awareness.

AS YOU KNOW, I'LL BE SPEAKING ABOUT gender mainstreaming.

TODAY WE ARE GOING TO LOOK AT this year's sales strategy.

THIS MORNING, I'D LIKE TO OUTLINE the concept we've
developed for you.

WELL, TODAY I'M GOING TO TELL YOU ABOUT THE IDEAS
WE'VE COME UP WITH FOR 2018.

BEFORE WE GET STARTED I'D LIKE TO TELL YOU SOMETHING
ABOUT the topic I intend to cover.

RIGHT, I WOULD LIKE TO BEGIN WITH some facts.

How to give a plan of your talk

Let me just to give you a brief overview to start with.

The first point I'd like to make is that it's my utmost pleasure to welcome you all here today.

So, my talk will be divided into two parts: First I'm going to look at our past performance and second I'm going to focus on this year's targets.

Let me start by saying that I've divided my presentation into three parts. Firstly, I'll give you an overview about our key targets. Secondly, I'll discuss how we could possibly reach them and finally, I'll talk you through the possible implementation of our plans.

Right, so my talk is in three parts. I'll start with the contract specifications move on to how they are to be implemented and finish off with a Q&A session.

Right, at this point, I'd like to give you a short overview of my presentation. I'm going to start with an introduction to intercultural studies. Then I'll deal with the issue of defining culture. After that I'll discuss the culture iceberg. I'll think we have time for a short break at that point. After the break, I'll move on to some case studies and at the end, I'll conclude with a few role plays. There will be time for discussion at the end.

How to invite questions

I'll take questions as we go.
If you have any questions, please don't hesitate to interrupt me.

Before I forget: Please feel free to interrupt me at any time, should you have any questions.

Please ask any questions as we go along if there's anything you're not clear about.

There'll be time for questions at the end.
Yes, and I'll be glad to answer any questions (at the end of my talk).

Let me just ask you if there are any questions you'd like to ask at this point.

So, are there any questions on any of that?
Does anyone have any questions?

How to refer to an interruption

I'll be saying more about this in a minute.

I guess that's an important point to be made here.
Thank you for this precious input.

14

HOW TO RESPOND TO A QUESTION

I'D LIKE TO RESPOND TO THE GENTLEMAN / LADY WHO ASKED IF I thought we were on the right way.

THANK YOU. I'M GLAD YOU RAISED THAT POINT.
I'M HAPPY TO ANSWER THAT ONE.

HOW TO DEFER AN ANSWER

I THINK WHAT YOU'RE REALLY ASKING ABOUT IS whether I believed our goal was achievable or not.

I'M AFRAID WE DON'T HAVE THE ANSWER TO THAT YET.

THIS IS A COMPLEX ISSUE AND WE DON'T HAVE THE TIME TO ADDRESS IT NOW. CAN WE GET BACK TO YOU ON THAT?

HOW TO DECLINE AN ANSWER

I'M AFRAID WE'RE CURRENTLY NOT IN A POSITION TO COMMENT ON THAT.

SORRY, I'M NOT AT LIBERTY TO COMMENT ON THAT.

How to give background information

Right, let me give you some background to start with.
Let's start with the background.
Let's just put this into some kind of perspective.

How to go into details

Right, I'd now like to look at this in more detail.
Perhaps I should expand on that a little.

Well, to say a bit more about that, I would like to mention that we founded our company 25 years ago and have been gradually expanding it since.

To give you an example of what I mean, let me tell you the following:...

How to refer to the audience's knowledge

As you certainly know we are here to discuss our sales strategy.
As you are probably well aware we have come here to inform you about this year's main objectives.

I'm sure the implications of this are clear to all of us.

How to change the topic

OK, LET'S NOW LOOK AT the next graph.
OK, LET'S MOVE ON.
RIGHT, LET'S MOVE ON TO our second point on the agenda.

TO MOVE ON TO MY NEXT POINT, LET ME ask you to look at my slide 5.
MOVING ON TO our next topic, I'd ask you to take a look at handout 8.

RIGHT, TO TURN TO A DIFFERENT MATTER NOW, let's listen to Martin's expertise about this legal issue.

OK, TO GO BACK TO WHAT I WAS SAYING, I strongly believe this campaign will be highly successful.

ALLOW ME TO DIGRESS FOR A MOMENT.

How to refer to visuals

NEXT, PLEASE HAVE A LOOK AT THIS.

AS YOU CAN SEE, the share prices were quite volatile last summer.

I'D LIKE TO POINT OUT THAT sales have increased since last May.

TO GIVE YOU THE BACKGROUND TO THIS, I WOULD LIKE TO SAY THAT the peak you can see in this graph coincides with the launch of our new product.

So, WHAT DOES THIS MEAN IN TERMS OF profit?
IF YOU LOOK AT THE GRAPH YOU WILL SEE THAT we've been on a bit
of a roller coaster ride recently.

IF YOU'D LIKE TO LOOK AT THE SCREEN, YOU'LL SEE how much
the situation has changed recently.

RIGHT, I'D NOW LIKE YOU TO LOOK AT THIS graph.
COULD I NOW DRAW YOUR ATTENTION TO the chart?

THE FIGURES CLEARLY SHOW a sharp decline in turnover.
WELL, AS YOU CAN SEE, THE FIGURES speak for themselves.

HOW TO ASK QUESTIONS AFTER A PRESENTATION

Gerald, I'VE GOT A QUESTION, IF YOU DON'T MIND.

IN YOUR TALK, YOU MENTIONED Chinese competitors. SORRY,
BUT COULD YOU EXPLAIN THAT TO ME IN MORE DETAIL, PLEASE?

SO, LET ME SEE IF I UNDERSTAND YOU CORRECTLY. YOU SAID THAT
we were facing fairly difficult times. IS THAT RIGHT?

I SEE. BUT why do you think so?

OK, BUT WHAT ABOUT fundraising?

MM, I'M AFRAID THAT DOESN'T REALLY MAKE SENSE TO ME.
WHY WOULD we want to do that?

JUST ONE MORE THING, PERHAPS you could provide us with
an example.

I SEE, THAT MAKES SENSE NOW. THANKS.

HOW TO CONCLUDE

SO, TO SUM UP, we have reached conclusions on the
following issues.

WELL, TO SUM UP, this language training has proved
quite successful.

TO SUMMARISE, I WOULD SAY THAT it has been a highly joyful event.

SO, LET ME CONCLUDE BY SAYING THAT I'm very happy with
the outcome of today's meeting.

WELL, SO ALLOW ME TO CONCLUDE BY HIGHLIGHTING THE FACT
THAT it is always great to see you all here.

IN FACT, I'D LIKE TO CONCLUDE BY STATING THAT this has been
a rather fruitful meeting again.

IN FACT, HAVING SAID THAT, THIS BRINGS ME TO THE END OF MY TALK.

FINALLY, MY ADVICE TO YOU ALL OF YOU HERE IS to reach for
the stars at all times.

How to end

Thanks very much. Are there any questions?

Well, that's all I have to say. Thank you very much for your attention.

Well, that's it from me. Thank you very much for listening.

How to describe graphs, charts and trends

(BbC and LAS stand for company names)

How to describe similarity

LOOKING AT THIS CHART, WE CAN SEE THAT BOTH SHARE PRICES INCREASED SHARPLY in November.

CONSIDERING ALL OF THE AVAILABLE INFORMATION, WE SEE THAT BbC ROSE AS SHARPLY AS LAS DID IN the first quarter of the year.

IT SEEMS THAT NEITHER COMPANY HAS MADE A PROFIT YET.

THIS GRAPH ILLUSTRATES THAT LIKE BbC, LAS ALSO FELL in June.

How to describe difference

BbC FELL SHARPLY WHEREAS LAS REMAINED STEADY IN the second quarter of the year.

SO FAR BbC HAS FALLEN RAPIDLY / DRAMATICALLY COMPARED TO LAS.

UNLIKE BbC, LAS HAS RISEN BY 10% SINCE 1 July.

BbC ROSE FAR MORE DRAMATICALLY THAN LAS DID last year.

How to contrast information

In contrast to 2010, 2011 seems rather promising.

Unlike Vienna Airways, London Airlines offer lots of bargains.

As opposed to Blueberry, MOD's is an Italian brand.

Whereas / while LAS is a programme focusing on Latin America, Business by Cultures isn't.

Sweet Suite Hotels **and** Charlston **differ in that** the latter offers special weekend bargains, whereas the former doesn't.

On the one hand I tend to fully support our sales department, **but on the other hand** I'm not entirely sure they always use the appropriate sales technique.

For one thing, I believe it's quite trendy **and for another,** I guess it might be a bestseller in the long run.

I believe it's not so much a question of time **as of** money.

If you ask me, it's more a question of solid work **than of** mere intuition.

Well, another way of looking at this is to see this change as a chance.

How to comment on graphs, charts and trends

What seems to be happening increasingly is a change
in spending habits.

I think the biggest effect has been caused by the recent merger.

**Looking at this more closely we are seeing a major change
in the way** our customers respond.

The danger I can now see is that our shares drop even further.

On balance, I'd say last year was not as successful as we had
expected it to be.

The fact is, it was slightly less successful than we had hoped
it would be.

So, all in all it was relatively successful in the end.

HOW TO NEGOTIATE

HOW TO START NEGOTIATING

HELLO AND WELCOME EVERYBODY. WE'RE LOOKING FORWARD TO A PRODUCTIVE MEETING.

HOW TO ASK FOR POSITIONS

SORRY, I WAS WONDERING IF YOU CAN TELL ME A LITTLE ABOUT your standing on this?

COULD YOU TELL ME/US WHAT YOU HAVE IN MIND?

WOULD YOU LIKE TO SET OUT YOUR requirements first?

WOULD YOU BE WILLING TO ACCEPT A COMPROMISE?
WOULD THAT COMPROMISE BE SATISFACTORY FOR YOU?

SO, Sarah, HOW DO YOU FEEL ABOUT THIS? ARE THESE TERMS BROADLY ACCEPTABLE?

Martin, IS THAT ACCEPTABLE FOR US AS A COMPROMISE SOLUTION?

RIGHT. SO WHAT SORT OF TIME-SCALE ARE WE LOOKING AT?

HOW TO STATE POSITIONS

PERHAPS WE COULD BEGIN BY OUTLINING OUR INITIAL POSITION.

IDEALLY, WE'D LIKE TO SEE unanimity.
WHAT WE'RE LOOKING FOR HERE IS the best solution for everyone.

WELL, TO BE HONEST, WE'D LIKE TO REACH a deal with you today.
WELL, TO BE HONEST, WE ARE HERE TO SEE some movement on price.

HOW TO MAKE OFFERS AND CONCESSIONS

WHAT IF WE OFFERED YOU AN ALTERNATIVE?

WELL, IF YOU sign the deal today, **WE CAN** start with production tomorrow.

WE'D BE ABLE TO offer you a better deal
IF YOU ordered a quantity of 1,000 straight away.

WE ARE PREPARED TO offer you better conditions
ON THE UNDERSTANDING THAT you will pay within one week.

WE ARE MORE THAN READY TO place major orders
AS LONG AS you offer us special conditions.

I THINK WE COULD supply you with excellent quality,
PROVIDED THAT YOU describe your requests in detail.

WE'D BE PREPARED TO make concessions, IF we can count on your
reliability.
WELL, WE MAY BE IN THE POSITION TO REVISE OUR OFFER.

WELL, I'M AFRAID WE COULD ONLY ACCEPT THIS ON ONE CONDITION.
WELL, I MUST SAY IF WE AGREED, IT WOULD BE CONDITIONAL ON
you placing a firm order.

TO BE HONEST, WE'D BE RELUCTANT TO do business with ERT again
UNLESS we get a written confirmation from them stating that
they'd fulfil all our requirements in time.

HONESTLY SPEAKING, WE STILL HAVE CERTAIN RESERVATIONS ABOUT
you meeting the deadline, AND UNLESS you provide us with
a written confirmation, WE'D rather do business with one
of your competitors instead.

HOW TO AVOID MISUNDERSTANDING

SO, ARE YOU SAYING you're going to Paris by train next time?

SORRY, WHAT EXACTLY DO YOU MEAN?
HAVE I GOT THIS RIGHT? WHAT YOU ARE SAYING IS THAT
our turnover has decreased by 5% since September?

SORRY, I'M NOT ENTIRELY WITH YOU. COULD YOU GIVE US
AN IDEA OF WHAT YOU'RE LOOKING FOR?
OK, LET ME JUST CHECK I UNDERSTAND YOU CORRECTLY.
YOU MEAN, IF WE ordered now you would grant us a discount?

IF I UNDERSTAND YOU CORRECTLY YOU THINK YOU/WE
have good chances to win the tender.

LET ME GET THIS QUITE CLEAR.
OK, LET'S JUST TIE UP A FEW LOOSE ENDS, SHALL WE?

HOW TO ASK FOR FURTHER INFORMATION

I'M SORRY, BUT COULD YOU BE A BIT MORE precise HERE?
SORRY, BUT I WAS WONDERING IF YOU COULD PROVIDE US WITH
some more details in this respect.

SORRY, BUT COULD YOU ELABORATE A BIT ON THAT, PLEASE?
I'M SORRY, BUT WOULD YOU MIND EXPLAINING THIS IN A LITTLE
MORE DETAIL?

HOW TO PLAY FOR TIME

I'M AFRAID THAT'S A RATHER DIFFICULT QUESTION TO ANSWER NOW.

YES, THAT'S A VERY INTERESTING QUESTION. CAN I GET BACK
TO YOU ON THAT?

YES, I CAN SEE YOUR POINT, BUT I THINK YOU WILL UNDERSTAND
HOW COMPLEX THIS ISSUE IS.

16

How to say nothing

Well, I'm afraid that's rather difficult to forecast at present.

I'm afraid I'm currently not in a position to provide you with further details just now.
I'm afraid I don't have enough information at my disposal to give you a satisfying answer.

I'm afraid we'd be running a bit short of time if we were to consider all the implications this aspect might bring about.

How to refuse an offer

I'm afraid I'm not sure about that.
I'm afraid that would be difficult for us.
I'm afraid you leave us with little alternative but to start all over again.

I'm afraid in that case, we would be virtually obliged to refuse your offer.
I'm afraid that's more than we usually pay.
I'm afraid having to say that this doesn't really solve our problem.
Well, I'm afraid I think that's about as far as we can go at this stage.
Well, to be honest, at the moment we do not see this as a viable option, I'm afraid.

HOW TO ACCEPT AN OFFER

RIGHT, WE SEEM TO BE NEARING AGREEMENT.
WELL, THAT SOUNDS A GOOD IDEA TO ME. AS LONG AS WE stick to
our mutual agreement, I can't see any problems coming up.

GOOD, SO WE AGREE ON price, quantity, discounts. THE DEAL IS MADE.

YES, I THINK THAT WOULD BE ACCEPTABLE FOR US.
YES, I MUST SAY THIS SEEMS TO BE a perfect compromise.

IF YOU ACCEPTED TO meet halfway, WE'D be prepared to accept
your offer.

HOW TO FINISH A ROUND OF NEGOTIATIONS

WELL, TO BE HONEST, I'D LIKE TO THINK ABOUT IT.
RIGHT, I THINK WE'VE COVERED EVERYTHING. THAT'S GREAT!
GREAT! WE'VE GOT A DEAL. FANTASTIC!

HOW TO FOLLOW UP THE DEAL

RIGHT, AND PLEASE LET ME KNOW IF THERE ARE ANY problems.
OK... AND IF THERE ARE any other points, I'll e-mail you. OK?
GREAT, I THINK THAT'S EVERYTHING. I THINK WE'VE EARNED
OURSELVES A DRINK, HAVEN'T WE?

17

HOW TO RUN A FORMAL MEETING

HOW TO OPEN A FORMAL MEETING

LADIES AND GENTLEMEN, I DECLARE THE MEETING OPEN.

HOW TO DEAL WITH THE MINUTES

HAS EVERYONE RECEIVED THE MINUTES?

CAN WE CONSIDER THE MINUTES AS READ?

ARE THERE ANY OBJECTIONS TO THE MINUTES?

HOW TO PRESENT THE AGENDA

JUST TO BE ON THE SAFE SIDE: HAS EVERYBODY RECEIVED A COPY
OF TODAY'S AGENDA?

AS YOU CAN SEE, THE FIRST ITEM ON TODAY'S AGENDA IS
the election of a new chairperson.

ARE THERE ANY OBJECTIONS TO ADDING A FURTHER ITEM TO THE AGENDA?

COULD item 3 **BE DELETED FROM THE AGENDA AT HAND?**

HOW TO PRESENT THE TOPIC OF THE MEETING

LET ME BRIEFLY INTRODUCE YOU TO TODAY'S TOPICS. FIRST, we are going to talk about our last year's sales figures.
MAY I FIRST DRAW YOUR ATTENTION TO item 6 on the agenda?
I SUGGEST FIRST looking at item 9.

HOW TO GIVE THE FLOOR

I WOULD NOW LIKE TO OFFER THE FLOOR TO Martin.
Gerald, **WOULD YOU LIKE TO TAKE THE FLOOR NOW?**
Karin, **THE FLOOR IS ALL YOURS.**

HOW TO TAKE THE FLOOR

EXCUSE ME. WITH THE CHAIR'S PERMISSION I WOULD LIKE TO POINT OUT THAT we still need to agree on a few topics today.

SORRY, BUT I'D LIKE TO TAKE UP THE POINT REGARDING our last year's performance IF I MAY.

HOW TO MOVE ON TO THE NEXT ITEM

WOULD ANYONE WISH TO ADD ANYTHING FURTHER BEFORE WE MOVE ON TO THE NEXT ITEM ON OUR AGENDA?

DOES ANYONE HAVE ANYTHING FURTHER TO ADD?

HOW TO DIRECT A FORMAL MEETING

I'M AFRAID WE HAVE SLIGHTLY DIVERTED FROM THE MAIN ISSUE. OUR QUESTION ACTUALLY IS not last year's, but this year's performance.

I'M AFRAID THIS SEEMS TO EXCEED OUR PROGRAMME A BIT: WHAT WE ARE HERE TO FIND OUT IS what priorities we need to focus on next year.

Mr Hanson, WOULD YOU MIND STICKING A BIT MORE CLOSELY TO THE SUBJECT PLEASE?

SORRY BUT CAN WE ALL GET BACK TO THE SUBJECT, PLEASE?

WE SEEM TO GET SIDETRACKED. WOULD YOU MIND FOCUSING ON THE MAIN ISSUE, PLEASE?

How to keep order

Sorry, but we can't all speak simultaneously. Martin, would you like to present your point first?

Sorry, Karin, may I remind you to address your remarks to the chair, please?

How to summarise a formal meeting

As we have finally come to the end of our meeting, I would briefly like to summarise the main decisions we have made: Firstly, we decided to elect a new chair. Secondly, we agreed on drafting the new guidelines. Thirdly, we adopted our formal procedures.

How to end a formal meeting

I would now like to seize the opportunity to thank you all for your esteemed attendance and active participation, the administrative staff for their excellent preparation of the meeting and the interpreters for their reliable service.

Thank you very much and good-bye—have a pleasant trip home.

I declare the meeting closed.

The Authors

Karin Ioannou-Naoum-Wokoun has a Master's degree in English and American Studies and Romance Languages. She is a trainer in Intercultural Conflict Management and International Business English and her client base includes many multinational companies. She also works as Business English coach for a variety of multinational companies and public institutions and translates films, contracts, textbooks and scientific publications.

Martin Helmuth von Ruelling holds a doctorate in European Law and a Master's degree in European Studies. He has worked as a lawyer specialising in European company law in Austria and Brazil and as as a lecturer in European Studies at the University EAFIT in Medellin, Colombia. He translates law-related and scientific texts from German to English and English to German and works as a consultant for a number of law firms.

Karin and Martin also run **Business by Cultures** together.
www.businessbycultures.org

Gerald Nestler is a visual artist and researcher. As part of his artistic research on economy and finance he worked as a broker and trader and co-founded companies in art consultancy as well as media art. He co-edited the issues 200 and 201 of the German art magazine KUNSTFORUM INTERNATIONAL on art and economy. He is a practice-based PhD candidate at Goldsmiths College, University of London. He teaches e.g. Management in the Arts at the Department of Art/Visual Culture, Webster University Vienna.